Note to Parents and Teachers

The READING ABOUT: STARTERS series introduces key science vocabulary and concepts to young children while encouraging them to discover and understand the world around them. The series works as a set of graded readers in three levels.

LEVEL 3: READ ALONE follows guidelines set out in the National Curriculum for Year 3 in schools. These books can be read alone or as part of guided or group reading. Each book has three sections:

• Information pages that introduce key concepts. Key words appear in bold for easy recognition on pages where the related science concepts are explained.
• A lively story that recalls this vocabulary and encourages children to use these words when they talk and write.
• A quiz asks children to look back and recall what they have read.

HOW FAR DOES IT STRETCH? looks at SPRINGS. Below are some answers and activities related to the questions on the information spreads that parents, carers and teachers can use to discuss and develop further ideas and concepts:

p. 6 *What objects in your home spring back into shape when you let them go?* Children could make a chart sorting objects into two groups: elastic and non-elastic.

p. 9 *Why does a folded strip of paper pop up when you let it go?* The folded paper works like a spring. Explain that springs can be made from different materials such as paper and plastic, but that some materials are more elastic than others, e.g. steel springs.

p. 13 *How is a clockwork spring different from other springs?* Clockwork springs are flat and spring sideways, unlike coiled springs that stretch and squash end to end. You could also describe leaf springs used on trucks and tractors that are flat and spring by bending in the middle – like a diving board. A paperclip is a kind of spring, too!

p. 15 *Can you feel the difference when you land bending your knees?* Bending our knees gives a softer landing. You could explain that all our muscles act like springs, e.g. they work by squashing and stretching. You could ask children to think of animals that can spring high into the air, e.g. grasshopper, kangaroo, flea (all with long legs!).

p. 16 *What happens if the boy pulls the elastic band harder?* The harder you pull, the more an elastic band stretches. But if you stretch the elastic band too far, it will break.

p. 19 *Which of these objects spring back again?* A ruler makes a "twanging" noise as it springs up and down. A guitar string makes a noise in the same way when it is plucked.

p. 21 *What happens to a bicycle tyre when you let the air out?* You could ask children if they have ever ridden on a flat tyre – it gives a very bumpy ride!

ADVISORY TEAM

Educational Consultant
Andrea Bright – Science Co-ordinator, Trafalgar Junior School, Twickenham

Literacy Consultant
Jackie Holderness – former Senior Lecturer in Primary Education, Westminster Institute, Oxford Brookes University

Series Consultants
Anne Fussell – Early Years Teacher and University Tutor, Westminster Institute, Oxford Brookes University

David Fussell – C.Chem., FRSC

CONTENTS

© Aladdin Books Ltd 2005

Designed and produced by
Aladdin Books Ltd
2/3 Fitzroy Mews
London W1T 6DF

First published in
Great Britain in 2005 by
Franklin Watts
96 Leonard Street
London EC2A 4XD

A catalogue record for this
book is available from the
British Library.

ISBN 0 7496 6251 4 (H'bk)

ISBN 0 7496 6386 3 (P'bk)

All rights reserved
Printed in Malaysia

Editor: Jim Pipe
Design: Flick, Book Design
and Graphics
Thanks to:
• The pupils of Trafalgar Junior
School, Twickenham and St.
Paul's C.E. Primary School,
Addlestone, for appearing as
models in this book.
• Ronan and Ciannait Khan
O'Donnell and Sarah O'Halloran
for appearing as models in the story.
• The pupils and teachers of
Trafalgar Junior School,
Twickenham and St. Nicholas
C.E. Infant School, Wallingford,
for testing the sample books.

• Andrea Bright, Janice Bibby and
Stephanie Cox for helping to
organise the photoshoots.

Photocredits:
*l-left, r-right, b-bottom, t-top,
c-centre, m-middle*
Cover tr, tl and b, 2tl & bl, 4 both,
5tr, 9 all, 10 both, 13 all, 16 both,
18tr, 19br, 22br, 31tr — Marc
Arundale /Select Pictures. Cover tm,
3, 7 both, 11 ml, 17, 22tr & mr,
23, 31bcr — Photodisc. 2ml, 5bl &
br, 6 all, 8 both, 11tr, 12 both, 14
mr, 21mr & bl, 22bc, 24tr & ml,
25 all, 26-27 all, 29 all, 30, 31ml,
br & bl — Jim Pipe. 5tr, 28tl, 31bcl
— PBD. 15mr, 18b — US Navy.
15br — DAJ. 20m, 21t — Corbis.
20bl — Digital Vision. 22mc, 24br
— Ingram Publishing.

SPRINGS

How Far Does It Stretch?

by Sally Hewitt

Aladdin/Watts
London • Sydney

SPRINGS

A **spring** is a long piece of wire or plastic which is coiled round and round.

You can push and squash it or pull and stretch it.

When you let go, it **springs** back into shape.

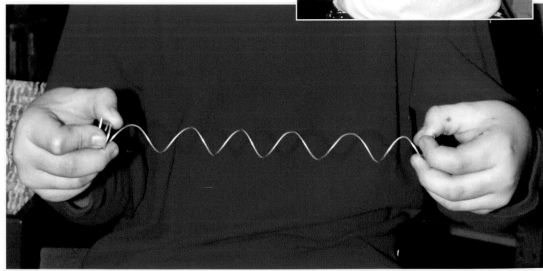

Stretch

Pushes and pulls are forces that make things move and change shape.

4

Springs are often hidden inside things you use every day.

Clothes pegs
A spring helps a clothes peg to grip the clothes on a washing line.

Sofa
Springs in a sofa squash when you sit down. They spring back again when you get up.

Toaster
The springs in a toaster make the toast pop up!

Smooth ride
Springs help trains, cars and bicycles to ride more gently over bumps.

ELASTIC

You squash and stretch things every day to change their shape.

You squash a sponge when you wash. You stretch a hair-band to tie up your hair.

The sponge and hair-band are made of **elastic** materials. They spring back into shape.

Squashing a sponge

Stretching a hair-band

Think about objects that you can squash or stretch, such as a cuddly toy, modelling clay or a balloon.

What objects in your home spring back into shape when you let them go?

Elastic material stops our socks and trousers from slipping off.

An **elastic** waistband stretches when you pull on your shorts.

Elastic material is good for sports clothes. Why do you think this is?

Elastic keeps a diver's mask on underwater.

Sports clothes

BOUNCING AND TUMBLING

Springs can make toys pop up, **bounce** and walk downstairs.

The spring in a pogo stick is very strong. You push down with your body to squash it.

The spring pushes up again and you **bounce** up and down!

Spring

The spring on this table football player makes it bounce off the sides of the table.

A Slinky toy is a spring that moves in an unusual way. It **tumbles** downstairs!

Pull one end of the Slinky and stretch it down to the next step. The top of the Slinky **tumbles** after it.

Fold a strip of paper back and forth to make a spring.

Cut out and stick on a frog shape. Press the frog down and then let it go. Why does it pop up?

9

SQUASHING SPRINGS

There are springs inside many of the things at school and at home.

A spring inside a ball-point pen pops the point in and out when you press the top.

Can you see the springs in this hole puncher?

You **squash** a spring when you press down on a stapler. It springs open when you let go.

Stapler

A spring inside a weighing scales is **squashed** when an object is put in the bowl. It makes a needle move round the dial.

A heavy object **squashes** the spring more, so the needle moves further.

Spring

Dial

On the front and back of trains are large springs called buffers.

When a train is joined to a carriage, the buffers are squashed and not the carriage!

Buffers

CLOCKWORK

Most modern clocks and watches use battery power to make them go. Older clocks use **clockwork**.

This clockwork egg timer works using a spring.

Clockwork uses a spring to make the clock go. You turn a key or knob to make the spring stretch.

As the spring goes back into shape, it turns the clock hands.

When the spring has gone back into shape, you have to wind the clock up again.

Spring

Clock

Moving toys are often powered by **clockwork**.

The key winds up the spring inside.

Winding up the spring

Key

As the spring unwinds it moves the legs or wheels, and the toy moves along.

A clockwork spring is flat. It is squashed and stretched sideways.

How is this different from other springs?

SHOCK ABSORBERS

Mountain bikes are built to jump over holes and bumps. Strong springs help to give the rider a soft landing!

The bike lands with a bump and squashes the springs. This sort of spring is called a **shock absorber**.

Bicycle spring

Monster truck

This monster truck has giant springs to help it bounce over cars!

Cars also have springs that are **shock absorbers**. These springs give a smooth ride.

Big springs can support a truck's heavy load.

Rubber tyres

Cars and bicycles also have rubber tyres. Rubber is an elastic material that squashes and stretches and goes back into shape.

Your knees are like springs. Make a small jump and land with your knees straight.

Now jump up and land bending your knees. Can you *feel* the difference?

15

ELASTIC BANDS

Elastic bands are a ring of elastic.
They stretch when you pull them.
They spring back when you let them go.

Elastic bands can stretch to different sizes. They are useful for holding things together.

Elastic band

What can be held together with elastic bands?

This boy is stretching an elastic band.
He can feel it pull on his fingers. What happens if he pulls the elastic band harder?

Bungee jump

Bungee jumps are ONLY done by adults with expert help.

Some adults do stunts like bungee jumping.
A bungee is like a huge **elastic band**.
One end is tied to the jumper.
The other end is tied to a bridge or crane.

When the person jumps, the bungee
stretches. When it is fully stretched, it
makes the jumper spring back up again!

CATAPULTS AND BOWS

An elastic band can make a **catapult**.

This boy has tied a strong elastic band between two nails.

He pulls back the elastic band with the car. When he lets go, the car shoots off!

How could he make the car move faster?

Catapult

The catapult on an aircraft carrier shoots jet planes into the air.

A **bow** is made of springy wood or plastic. It bends when the string is pulled back.

When the archer lets go of the string, the **bow** makes the string spring back and push the arrow through the air.

Bow

Hold a wooden ruler, a plastic biro and a metal spoon over the edge of a table.

Then press down on the end of each object and let go. Which of these objects spring back again?

INFLATABLES AND TRAMPOLINES

An **inflatable** is made of an elastic material. It is full of air to make it extra bouncy.

If this **inflatable** boat hits a rock, it just bounces off!

Inflatable boat

When this girl bounces down on the **inflatable** ball, it springs back and bounces her up again.

Inflatable ball

Trampoline

Springs *and* elastic make a **trampoline** extra bouncy.

The harder you land on a **trampoline**, the higher you fly up into the air.

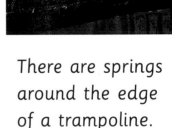

There are springs around the edge of a trampoline.

Air can be let out of an inflatable ball. Without air inside it, the ball isn't bouncy.

What happens to a bicycle tyre when you let the air out?

BALLS

Bouncy **balls** are made of elastic material such as plastic or rubber and filled with air.

The **ball** squashes when it hits the ground. It goes back into shape and bounces up again.

Ball squashes as it hits ground

A basketball is made for bouncing.

Would all these balls bounce well if you dropped them?

Basketball

Pool balls

Marble

Tennis ball

Trainers

Why do people wear trainers for **ball** games?

The rubber soles of trainers bend, squash and stretch to help athletes run, jump and bounce. They give a soft landing like shock absorbers.

23

IS IT BOUNCY?

Look out for words about springs and elastic materials.

Erin and Sara were bouncing on their beds. They weren't allowed to!

Erin was bigger and heavier than Sara. She bounced the highest. "Hey! No bouncing on the beds!" said Dad.

The children went downstairs. "This sofa is bouncy, too," said Sara. "No bouncing on the sofa either!" said Dad.

Sara tried bouncing on the floor. Dad laughed, "You look like a little kangaroo!"

"Why isn't the ground bouncy
like the bed?" asked Sara.
"Because beds have springs
inside them," said Dad.

"Let's go outside," said Erin.
"My pogo stick has got a spring."
Erin bounced up and down
on her pogo stick.

"The ground is bouncy now!"
said Sara.
"The ground isn't bouncy," said Dad,
"but the spring in
the pogo stick is."

Dad tried next. He bounced
so high he flew right off!

"I want a go!" said Sara.
Sara couldn't bounce very
high on the pogo stick.

"It's not fair!" wailed Sara. "Why won't it bounce for me?"

"You're not heavy enough to squash the spring," said Dad.

Sara started to cry. "Let's blow up your inflatable ball," said Dad.

"It hasn't got springs! So why is it bouncy?" asked Sara.

"It is made of stretchy material, like elastic." said Erin. "And it's full of air."

"What's elastic?" asked Sara.

Erin took off Sara's hair-band. "This is elastic," she said. "Look, it stretches and springs back into shape. We're learning about it at school."

Soon Sara was bouncing up and down on the inflatable ball. "This is even more bouncy than the bed," she laughed.

"Watch out for that sharp stick," shouted Dad.

Too late!
The stick made a hole in the inflatable.
"All the air is rushing out," said Erin.

"Feel it now," said Sara ."Without air inside it, the inflatable isn't bouncy."

"Don't worry," said Dad, "I know somewhere that's really bouncy."

"Yippee! Let's go!" shouted Sara and Erin.

They all climbed into the car. "A car has springs too," said Dad.
"Just like the springs on Erin's bike."

"Springs help a car to drive smoothly on the road."
"You can feel them when we go over a bump."

At the park, they ran over to the trampoline.
"The trampoline has got springs!" said Sara.

"And stretchy elastic too! We can bounce up to the moon!" said Erin.

They watched a girl bouncing on the trampoline.

The trampoline stretched down, sprang back and pushed her into the air.

The girl's big sister bounced even higher! The elastic in the bungee straps stretched when she went down. But it pulled her high into the air.

"Let's go to the bouncy castle first," said Dad.
Erin and Sara ran to the bouncy castle.
They took off their shoes and jumped on.

The girls tried the bouncy castle. Then they went on the trampoline.

"This is the bounciest thing of all!" shouted Sara. She bounced harder and harder and higher and higher.

Dad look worried. "Not too high," he said. "You might bounce right off into space!"

WRITE YOUR OWN STORY about things that bounce. Or you can make a list of elastic objects and things with springs in your home or at school. You could do a drawing to show where the springs or elastic are.

Springs	Elastic
Clothes peg	Sports socks
Sofa	Hair-band
Bed	Elastic band
Toy car	Swimsuit
Hair clip	Bathing cap

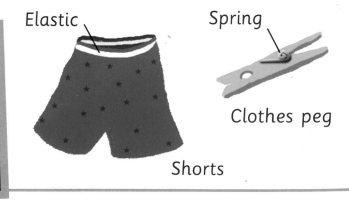

Elastic

Shorts

Spring

Clothes peg

QUIZ

You can squash or stretch a spring. What happens to a spring when you let it go?

Answer on pages 4 and 10-11

Sponges and hair-bands are made of elastic material. What is special about elastic material?

Answer on page 6-7

How does a bow make an arrow fly through the air?

Answer on page 21

Why are these objects bouncy?

Trampoline   Sofa   Inflatable

Pogo stick

Answers on pages 5, 8, 21

INDEX